Secrets

of the

Lost City

A Scientific Adventure in the
Honduran Rain Forest

SANDRA MARKLE

MILLBROOK PRESS / MINNEAPOLIS

For Steve Elkins and all the creative, courageous people who lived this adventure

Acknowledgments
The author would like to thank the following people for sharing their enthusiasm and expertise: Dr. Juan C. Fernandez-Diaz, the National Center for Airborne Laser Mapping, University of Houston, Houston, Texas; Steve Elkins, Lost City Project and Expedition Leader, Partner UTL Productions, Los Angeles, California; Dr. Christopher T. Fisher, Colorado State University and National Geographic Explorer, Fort Collins, Colorado; Travis W. King, Mammal Spatial Ecology and Conservation Lab, Washington State University, Pullman, Washington; Dr. Trond Larsen, Director, Rapid Assessment Program at Conservation International, Washington, DC; Dr. John Polisar, Coordinator of Wildlife Conservation Society Jaguar Program and Smithsonian Mason School of Conservation, Fairfax, Virginia; Manfredo A. Turcios-Casco, Instituto de Conservación Forestal, Tegucigalpa, Honduras; and Tom Weinberg, President, Media Burn Video Archive, Chicago, Illinois.

A special thank-you to Skip Jeffery for his loving support during the creative process.

Millbrook Press™
An imprint of Lerner Publishing Group, Inc.
241 First Avenue North
Minneapolis, MN 55401 USA

For reading levels and more information, look up this title at www.lernerbooks.com.

Illustrations on pages 5 and 9 by Laura K. Westlund.

Designed by Danielle Carnito.
Main body text set in Johnston ITC Std.
Typeface provided by International Typeface Corporation.

Library of Congress Cataloging-in-Publication Data

Names: Markle, Sandra, author.
Title: Secrets of the lost city : a scientific adventure in the Honduran rain forest / Sandra Markle.
Description: Minneapolis : Millbrook Press, 2022. | Series: Sandra Markle's science discoveries | Includes bibliographical references and index. | Audience: Ages 9–12 | Audience: Grades 4–6 | Summary: "Follow along on scientific expeditions to a remote area of the Honduran rain forest where an ancient city once stood. Discover artifacts as well as incredible animals that are flourishing there free from human influence" —Provided by publisher.
Identifiers: LCCN 2021051847 (print) | LCCN 2021051848 (ebook) | ISBN 9781728436593 (library binding) | ISBN 9781728445403 (ebook)
Subjects: LCSH: Mosquitia (Nicaragua and Honduras)—History—Juvenile literature. | Mosquitia (Nicaragua and Honduras)—Antiquities—Juvenile literature. | Rain forest animals—Mosquitia (Nicaragua and Honduras)—Juvenile literature.
Classification: LCC F1509.M9 M37 2022 (print) | LCC F1509.M9 (ebook) | DDC 972.85—dc23/eng/20211109

LC record available at https://lccn.loc.gov/2021051847
LC ebook record available at https://lccn.loc.gov/2021051848

Manufactured in the United States of America
1-49624-49554-3/10/2022

CONTENTS

The Big Mystery

Why in the world would anyone go to a place where the land is so rugged it's nearly impossible to travel, the wildlife is likely to kill you, and if you survive, you have a good chance of getting a terrible disease? But what if going there means you have a chance to unearth an amazing treasure? And to have the thrill of discovering something no one else could find?

For a very long time, both of those reasons compelled people to risk their lives searching Honduras's La Mosquitia rain forest. The goal was to find the ruins of the legendary Lost City Native peoples called Ciudad Blanca (White City in Spanish).

What's known of this Lost City comes from the stories passed down through generations by the Honduran Pech and Tawahka peoples. They spoke of a city that was struck by catastrophe and everyone living there fled. The stories of the Lost City intertwine with tales from the 1500s about Spanish conquistador Hernán Cortés's failed search for a Central American city full of gold. So, the Lost City was imagined to be full of treasure. These stories warned that anyone who finds the Lost City and takes anything away will soon have something terrible happen to them. But even that threat can't overcome the double lure of possibly finding treasure and being the one to find the famed Lost City in La Mosquitia.

Steve Elkins (*left*) and an expedition team that included Douglas Preston (*center*), Honduran soldiers, and a number of others went into La Mosquitia in search of the legendary Lost City in 2015.

Introduction to La Mosquitia

La Mosquitia is the largest tropical wilderness in Central America. Covering 20,000 square miles (51,800 sq. km) along the easternmost part of Honduras and extending into Nicaragua, it's far from any cities and spreads across incredibly challenging terrain. This includes lush swamps, fast-flowing rivers, roaring waterfalls, rugged mountains, deep ravines, grassy savannas, and forests so dense sunlight barely penetrates. As if all of this doesn't make the area challenging enough, La Mosquitia receives, on average, 10 feet (3 m) of rainfall a year. Besides fueling intense plant growth, this rain causes flooding and landslides. It also turns dirt into mud so fluid that anyone stepping in it sinks deep. And La Mosquitia is infested with venomous snakes, including the most dangerous venomous snake in Central America—the fer-de-lance. Bites from the rain forest's sand flies are also likely to inject parasites, causing leishmaniasis (leesh-muh-NEYE-uh-sis)—a disease that can cause sores on the skin or damage to internal organs.

In fact, it is La Mosquitia's extreme wildness and dangers, rather than laws or barriers, that have kept it largely uninhabited and unexplored.

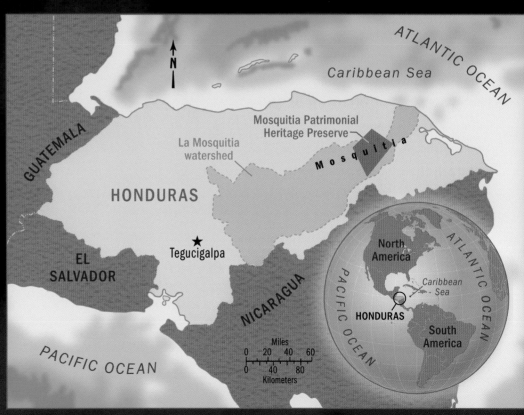

La Mosquitia was named for the Miskito people native to the area.

The Long Search

Although many unreported expeditions may have taken place, the earliest records of treks into La Mosquitia in search of the Lost City date from 1924 through 1934. These expeditions located some archaeological sites, or physical remains of people living there in the ancient past, and recovered pottery and tools. But no one on those expeditions believed they had discovered Ciudad Blanca. That's because no golden treasure was found. And the sites weren't built of white stones, which was how the stories described the famous Lost City. The public wasn't very excited about searches for an ancient city in La Mosquitia until a 1940 expedition by US explorer Theodore Morde.

Morde spent four months in the wild Honduran rain forest and returned with a collection of thousands of stone artifacts, or human-made objects. He also claimed he'd seen evidence of gold, silver, and platinum in the area where he'd found a ruined, walled city. Could he have discovered the legendary Ciudad Blanca? As intriguing as that was, the story Morde said his Native guides told him *really* grabbed people's attention. He reported the city supposedly once housed a temple with a staircase leading to a stone statue of a monkey god. US newspapers jumped on this story, calling the discovery the City of the Monkey God. Morde told no one how to find this city but vowed to return in 1941 to claim its treasures.

Left: This drawing by Virgil Finlay, titled *Lost City of the Monkey God*, illustrated the story of Theodore Morde's amazing discovery when it was first reported in the *American Weekly* newspaper supplement on September 22, 1940.

Below: Theodore Morde (May 18, 1911–June 26, 1954) was an explorer, US Army spy, reporter, radio announcer, and television news producer.

But things did not go as planned. World War II (1939–1945) was underway, and instead of returning to Honduras the following year, Morde went to Europe, serving as a spy for the US Army. Even after the war, Morde never went back to La Mosquitia. What happened? In 2016 author Douglas Preston read Morde's expedition journals, and he found that Morde's stories about finding the Lost City were false. The journal entries showed that Morde spent much of his time in Honduras illegally searching for gold. To cover this up, he and a partner dug up or purchased artifacts from local people at the end of the expedition.

It would be many years before Morde's sighting of a lost city that supposedly held the possibility of treasure in La Mosquitia was discovered to be fake. And, in that time, more hopeful searchers made expeditions to look for it, including ones in 1953, 1960, 1976, and 1985. There were several more failed expeditions in the 1990s, including a 1994 exploration by US documentary filmmaker Steve Elkins.

Anyone on an expedition in search of the Lost City in La Mosquitia quickly learned it wasn't an easy walk in the woods.

Although Elkins didn't find the Lost City, he made an amazing discovery. While on a tributary of the Río Plátano, he discovered a giant boulder with an intriguing carving. It showed a figure of a man wearing a headdress and carrying a bag over his shoulder that had seeds falling out of it. Looking at that boulder convinced Elkins there were things yet to be discovered in this intensely challenging rain forest. And he was certain that included the Lost City. Steve Elkins said, "I became obsessed with finding it."

Over the next four years, he made a few more expeditions into La Mosquitia—each unsuccessful.

So, in 1998, when Hurricane Mitch struck Honduras, canceling another planned trip, Elkins decided to give up on expeditions. But he *never* gave up thinking about the Lost City.

Then, twelve years later, in 2010, Steve Elkins heard about a team of researchers using a technology called lidar (light detection and ranging). The equipment had been put on board a plane and flown over the Belize rain forest to map an ancient Mayan city. He wondered, Could lidar mapping La Mosquitia show where to find the Lost City?

During Steve Elkins's 1994 expedition, an amazing carving was discovered on a boulder. Outlining it with chalk made it easy to see.

How Does Lidar Work?

To create a lidar map of an area, a low-flying plane carrying the lidar equipment makes repeated back-and-forth paths similar to the way someone usually mows a lawn.

- Every second the machine shoots out hundreds of thousands of laser pulses. The machine records the time between when the pulses shoot out and when the bounced-back reflections are received. It's like bouncing a ball on the ground and measuring the time it takes to bounce back.

- The lidar equipment measures the laser pulse bounce based on the constant speed of light. That sets the precise distance between the device in the plane to whatever bounced back the laser pulse.

- Meanwhile, the onboard navigation system (GPS and other special instruments) records the precise location on Earth that the plane and lidar equipment are over when that reflection is received.

- Later, a computer running a specialized program interprets that location and distance data to create a 3D map. This map is called a point cloud map, and it shows every reflected laser pulse.

A skilled operator is able to use other specialized computer programs to eliminate all the random-looking points—those are ones bounced off tree branches and leaves. Then the computer generates a 3D map that shows only the ground's contours and the shapes of any structures that were built on top of it.

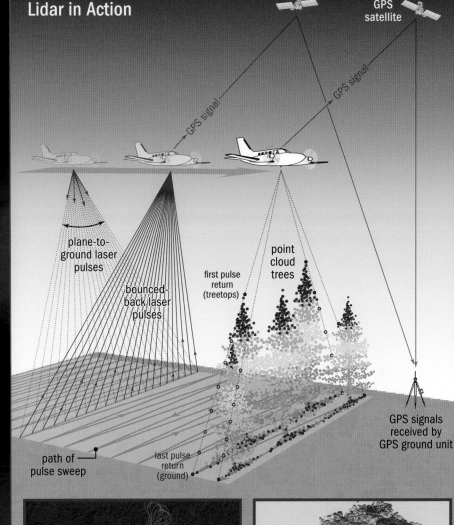

Lidar in Action

GPS satellite

GPS signal

GPS signal

plane-to-ground laser pulses

bounced-back laser pulses

point cloud trees

first pulse return (treetops)

path of pulse sweep

last pulse return (ground)

GPS signals received by GPS ground unit

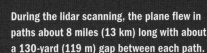

During the lidar scanning, the plane flew in paths about 8 miles (13 km) long with about a 130-yard (119 m) gap between each path.

This is the point cloud map of one lidar-scanned section of La Mosquitia.

Seeing through the Trees

Lidar mapping could reveal what was on the ground in La Mosquitia, but it was very expensive. So, Elkins decided to map only three small, close-together areas—about 50 square miles (129 sq. km). He chose the first target area, T1, which covered 20 square miles (52 sq. km) because it caught his attention on satellite images of La Mosquitia. It was a valley surrounded by steep, high mountains except for where a river cut through, limiting the way in and out. That would have made the valley easy to defend, and the river would have been a reliable water supply. There was also no record of anyone exploring that deep in the rain forest. He chose two other nearby sites, T2 and T3, as backups if T1 showed no signs of an ancient city.

But even this limited lidar mapping of La Mosquitia would be expensive as would any expedition to the site. As a film producer, Elkins decided to look for investors with the goal of creating a documentary about this search for the Lost City. His friend Tom Weinberg was happy to partner with him as was his friend and fellow film producer Bill Benenson.

People had tried flying over La Mosquitia in airplanes to search for the Lost City and failed to see it because the rain forest canopy was so dense.

Choosing where to lidar map, raising the funds to do it, and getting permission to map from the Honduran government had all taken time. So, the lidar mapping of the three target sites didn't begin until April 2012. Elkins, Weinberg, Benenson, a film crew, a support team, and Michael Sartori, a data-mapping scientist from the National Center for Airborne Laser Mapping, the group that would do the mapping, arrived on the island of Roatán in Honduras. This site was close to La Mosquitia and would be the base for the mapping operation. Next, pilot Chuck Gross and lidar operator Juan Fernandez-Diaz, also from the mapping center, arrived with the lidar equipment in the Cessna 337 Skymaster that would fly the mapping missions.

A computer-colored 3D map of the ground's surface made it easy to spot human-made structures since they were unnaturally boxy shapes.

Mapping T1 was first. It was a slow process, requiring three days of six to ten hours of flying dozens of back-and-forth parallel crossings at about 2,500 feet (762 m) above the ground—as low as it was possible to fly over the rain forest safely. This would be repeated over T2 and T3. But Sartori didn't want to wait for all three sites to be scanned before seeing any results. On the afternoon scanning T1 finished, he immediately started to turn the lidar data into a point cloud map. Then he used special computer programs to transform the point cloud map into 3D images that showed only the ground's surface. This work took Sartori all night, but the results were astounding! After seeing the 3D images, Elkins said, "There they were—boxy shapes that must be man-made around what had to be a city plaza."

Had they discovered Ciudad Blanca?

Only Way to Know

To know for certain if they'd found the remains of the long searched for Lost City, the team needed to ground truth the area—actually go into the T1 valley and look around. But organizing an expedition deep into La Mosquitia wasn't easy and took years. First, Elkins and his partners required the Honduran government's permission to both explore and to film there because they were still planning to create a documentary. Permission was eventually granted but only if soldiers went along to protect them.

It also took time to acquire the necessary camping equipment and hire helicopter transportation—the safest and fastest way into the T1 valley. But most of all, it took time to line up the best possible people for the expedition, starting with a film crew, National Geographic photographer Dave Yoder and journalist Douglas Preston, and several ex-British Special Air Service (SAS) soldiers to choose the campsite and help the explorers safely navigate the extreme terrain. Lidar expert Fernandez-Diaz would also accompany the explorers to make sure the special combined lidar and GPS units worked to locate the mapped possible archaeological sites on the ground.

As peaceful as the T1 valley looked from the air, it was full of dangers. The Honduran government insisted on soldiers accompanying the expedition to protect the explorers from dangerous wildlife, such as jaguars, and in case drug traffickers were operating in that remote part of La Mosquitia.

Team members were ferried, a few at a time, by helicopters from El Aguacate Airport, a rough, little airstrip carved out of the rain forest, to a small open area along the river in T1. Then they waded across to enter the forest.

Since this would be a scientific expedition as well as a discovery mission, it also needed a team of experts and their assistants to identify, study, and preserve whatever remains of the Lost City were found. Key among this group was anthropologist Alicia Gonzalez and archaeologists Oscar Neil Cruz, Chris Fisher, and graduate student Anna Cohen.

Finally, on February 16, 2015, the expedition was launched. Due to the cost and limited availability of helicopter flights, the explorers and scientists had just ten days to find the Lost City—if it was there.

The expedition team set up camp where, according to the computer-generated map of the T1 valley, they should be only about a quarter mile (0.4 km) from the boxy shapes believed to be the Lost City ruins. From their campsite, however, all the explorers could see was rain forest. Overhead in the trees, spider monkeys ran, screeching, while howler monkeys roared. Once it was dark, the group heard all sorts of eerie sounds from the wildlife in the forest. Lots of insects, especially mosquitoes, also appeared, swarming around the camp's glowing lanterns. Then someone almost stepped on a deadly fer-de-lance snake. This spot in La Mosquitia was clearly a very wild place. It was also unique. Fisher reported, "It's the only place I've ever been that there wasn't any plastic anywhere. And I've worked at archaeological sites in Europe, North America, and Latin America."

Throughout the search area, massive tree trunks supported a canopy of branches so thick even the middle of the day was twilight dark.

Exciting Discovery

No one slept well that first night deep in La Mosquitia. Their restlessness was partly due to the noisy, wild environment. But it was also because they knew they could be close to an amazing discovery. So, on the morning after their arrival, the eager group launched its search.

The going wasn't easy. They had to wade across a stream, plod through knee-deep mud, and struggle up a steep, slippery-wet, plant-covered hill. At the top of that hill, according to the lidar map displayed on the special GPS device Fisher carried, they should find the boxy, likely human-made structures.

What they discovered by pulling back dangling vines and brushing away dirt where Fisher pointed was walls of stacked boulders—which could have once been foundations for buildings. That was all they found that first day. And they found only more stone remnants of ancient architecture on the second day.

Oscar Neil Cruz used the rope the former British SAS soldiers anchored at the top to pull himself up the steep slope. This was the last obstacle to reaching the Lost City site. National Geographic reporter Douglas Preston (*in blue*) was right behind Cruz.

Elkins admitted, "I was disappointed. It's not like there was the Taj Mahal right in front of me."

But Fisher remained excited. He reported, "To my trained eye, I could tell we were looking at a city that was once just as monumental and fabulous as any Mayan city. Here, though, because what they had to build with was earth and wood instead of stone, the buildings didn't last." Centuries of weathering had slowly washed away any mud plaster and rotted away any wooden structures.

Elkins understood this but remained disappointed because nothing he saw was going to deliver that WOW moment of discovery for the documentary they were filming. But that was about to change.

While one of the SAS soldiers hacked a path through thick foliage, Chris Fisher (*left*) paused to check the GPS device and identify the next possible building location.

The tired explorers had just given up on the third day of the expedition and were trudging back to camp when a cameraman on the film crew called out. He shouted for the group to check some funny-looking rocks he'd stumbled over. Once these were carefully dug out of the dirt, ferns, and tree roots, they proved to be stone and ceramic artifacts. These varied from palm-sized items to objects so big they were hard for two people to lift. They included statues, bowls, vases, and stone stools. One of these stools was particularly striking because it had the carved head of a supernatural-looking jaguar on it. Jaguars are the largest cat native to the Americas.

The expedition team hadn't found gold, but the ancient artifacts were definitely a treasure. And the explorers were thrilled to have discovered a previously unknown city deep in La Mosquitia. Fisher reported, "Ciudad Blanca was possibly only ever a legend, but this city was real." Based on the discovery of the jaguar

The team discovered a carved were-jaguar head (a sculpture that appeared half human and half cat), slightly bigger than a softball, sticking out of the ground. When excavated, it was on one end of a stone stool.

stool, he encouraged the expedition team to name the site City of the Jaguar when they reported its discovery. Later, the Honduran government officially gave it that name. But to the explorers and to most Hondurans, the discovered site was called the Lost City and imagined to be the possible remains of Ciudad Blanca.

More important than the city's name or whether this really was the ruins of Ciudad Blanca was what the explorers found there. Thanks to his training, Fisher could look at the ruins in the rain forest and envision what the area had looked like when people lived in the city.

He said, "I estimate around ten thousand people lived there because of the number of mounds arranged around what were clearly [city] plazas." He believed those mounds were probably the sites of special city buildings. The terraces around the settlement, he thought, were home sites. He also found what he believed had been a city water reservoir behind the settlement and what were once canals that probably irrigated fields of food crops.

Fisher added, "While the City of the Jaguar is spectacularly isolated now, at its heyday, it was probably a center of trade and commerce." In studying the lidar maps of T2 and T3, he had spotted what he believed were the nearby remains of as many as nineteen other cities of unknown size largely covered by the rain forest.

Scientists, explorers, and film crew gathered to celebrate and talk about what they'd discovered.

Dig Deeper

As the discovery expedition was wrapping up, Fisher was already planning a return trip to the site. Once home, he and a number of the expedition members developed leishmaniasis symptoms and had to undergo treatment. Fisher, however, remained eager to go back. He wanted to excavate and study more artifacts before any were removed for public displays or news of the discovery led to people traveling to the site and stealing artifacts to sell. He knew the position and arrangement of artifacts at a site are a big part of what they reveal about the past. So, in 2016, Fisher went back for about a month, heading up a joint American-Honduran team of trained specialists with financial support from the National Geographic Society and the aid of Honduran soldiers.

During the original expedition, only the objects that were found protruding from the ground were uncovered. But while digging deeper into that site during the second expedition, Chris Fisher's team discovered much more—a total of about four hundred objects. Some were whole, and others were just broken bits.

This time, after studying the objects excavated at the Lost City site, Fisher estimated that they dated back to what archaeologists call the Mesoamerican postclassic period based on the carvings on the artifacts. That meant they were from around one thousand years ago. And what an amazing story they revealed about the past!

The sculpture of the vulture was significant because in Central American lore, it was said this bird could cross from the earthly world to a heavenly one.

The artifacts, including forty stone stools, were arranged in a circle on a bed of red clay around a central statue of what appeared to be a vulture. Fisher said, "We believe these [artifacts] represent a ritual closing of the [city] site." He explained that it was what archaeologists call a termination deposit. It was believed to have been made by the city's residents before they abandoned what had been their home—possibly fleeing a terrible pandemic.

Before leaving the excavation site for the second time, Fisher supervised the team's removal of a small number of artifacts and reburying of the others. While only about 200 square feet (19 sq. m) of the site had been studied, Fisher decided not to return again after some of his students who had accompanied him on the expedition became ill with leishmaniasis. He said, "As much as I'd like to, I couldn't promote any more [archaeological] work at the site. The threat of leishmaniasis makes being there too dangerous."

Despite all the challenges deep in La Mosquitia, another expedition would soon arrive in search of the Lost City's wildest secrets.

Send in the RAP Team

On February 14, 2017, two years after the discovery expedition and about a year after the archaeology expedition, another expedition to the Lost City site in La Mosquitia launched. This time, the explorers were a Conservation International Rapid Assessment Program (RAP) team. They'd come because this was one of the last remaining unexplored areas in Central America, and evidence suggested it had been undisturbed by people for many hundreds of years.

The RAP team had come as an ecological SWAT team for Conservation International to assess the health of this part of La Mosquitia. They hoped to make a case for increased monitoring and protection of the

Members of the RAP team

Travis King

John van Dort

Arnulfo Medina-Fitoria

Olvin W. Oyuela Andino

Milton Salazar-Saavedra

Eric van den Berghe

Onan Reyes

Manfredo A. Turcios-Casco

Trond Larsen

John Polisar

Carlos Funes

Josué Ramos Galdamez

Lost City site. It was a critical mission in an extremely difficult environment. But RAP team leader Trond Larsen was a wildlife biologist used to such challenges. The twelve scientists in this team were experts in their fields, veterans of working in extreme environments, and specialists in recognizing both plants and animals identified as endangered by the International Union for Conservation of Nature (IUCN). Team members included Onan Reyes (plants), Travis King (large mammals), John van Dort (birds), Eric van den Berghe (orchids, fish, butterflies, moths, and arthropods, such as spiders), Arnulfo Medina-Fitoria (bats), Manfredo A. Turcios-Casco (assistant for large and small mammals, reptiles, amphibians, and plants), Olvin W. Oyuela

Andino (plants), Milton Salazar-Saavedra (reptiles and amphibians), John Polisar (large mammals), Carlos Funes (birds), and Josué Ramos Galdamez (reptiles and amphibians).

Due to limited funding for supplies and helicopter transportation, the RAP team, like the earlier expeditions, had only limited time on-site. They had just eleven days to investigate every plant and animal they could find. They did have an advantage in being able to use the campsite already cleared by the earlier

In addition to tents for sleeping, the team had a kitchen area where they stacked their supplies.

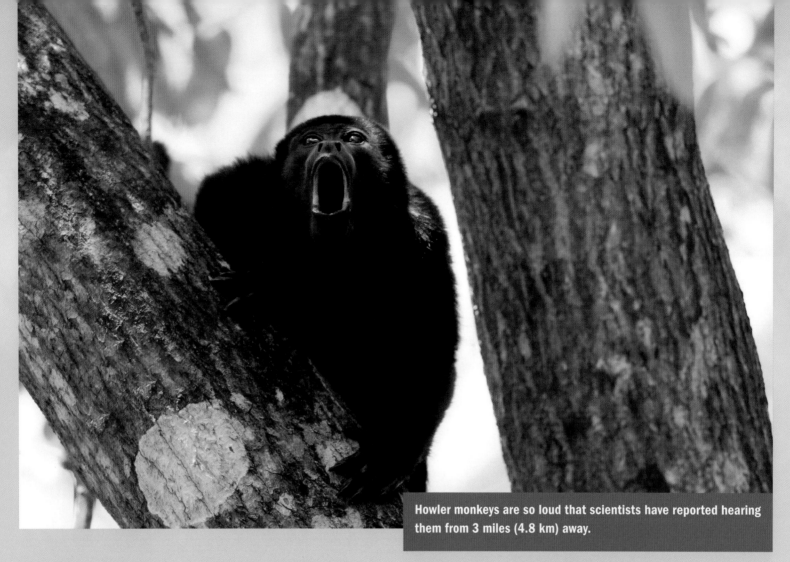

Howler monkeys are so loud that scientists have reported hearing them from 3 miles (4.8 km) away.

expeditions. And they had the support of a group of Honduran soldiers who were assigned to protect and help them. They could also use paths that had been hacked through the thick vegetation by the most recent archaeology expedition and were still somewhat clear.

Like the earlier explorers, the RAP team was greeted by spider monkeys screeching in overhead branches. Several of the scientists stopped to observe them. Larsen, whose specialty was insects, quickly spotted some beetles to study at the campsite. The spicy scent in the air made van den Berghe want to find the blooming flowers supplying this perfume. The RAP team was eager to start exploring as soon as it was light the next morning.

Alarm clocks weren't needed in the rain forest because the howler monkeys regularly roared at dawn and dusk. The monkeys also howled at other times to remind the scientists they were intruders in the rain forest. Wherever the scientists went, they explored with the precision and determination of a forensic team at a crime scene, and they always worked in small groups. A larger overall area could have been investigated if every scientist worked alone, or with just an assistant. But to be safe, they always worked in groups accompanied by a couple of soldiers.

While beautiful, the rain forest was packed with dangers, including rugged terrain, thorny plants, bullet ants whose sting was as painful as being shot, venomous snakes, and big cat predators—both jaguars and pumas. Large mammal scientist King said, "I did run into quite a few jaguar tracks, especially when I was following previously made [animal] pathways through the forest."

The teams, such as this one of Travis King (*left*), always explored the area accompanied by an assistant and soldiers. They systematically headed out from camp along one of the compass directions: north, south, east, or west.

The Search Party

As they explored, the RAP team focused on thoroughly examining each of the many different La Mosquitia environments, including swampy areas, streams, banks along streams, fern-covered spaces under giant trees, hilltops, and areas alongside waterfalls. At each site, the scientists collected plants and examined the animals they found. They worked both during the day and at night because some animals were only active at certain times. They recorded animal voices both day and night because the rain forest was always full of the sounds of its diverse wildlife.

Above: Botanist Onan Reyes could get a close look at only a very limited number of orchids in the forest because most grew high up in the very tall trees.

Left: At night Olvin W. Oyuela Andino preserved plants to study back home in his lab while insects swarmed in the camp light.

Below: Male harlequin beetles, such as this one found at the Lost City site, have superlong front legs, which they use to fight for a female to mate.

Some sounds were soft, such as buzzing insects. Others were medium loud, such as piglike peccaries woofing and grunting. Still other noises were even louder, such as the raspy calls of great green macaws and, of course, the roars of howler monkeys.

The scientists spent many hours watching and photographing all kinds of plants and animals from snakes and turtles to birds, deer, and peccaries. But they were careful never to interfere with wildlife going about their lives. For Polisar and King that meant just watching even when they came across two animals locked in a fierce struggle!

Above: Trond Larsen's discovery of this beautiful morpho butterfly at the Lost City site was exciting because these butterflies are becoming rare elsewhere in the world.

Right: A white sheet and battery-powered fluorescent or mercury vapor lights let Eric van den Berghe attract and catch the nighttime flying insects he identified and studied.

An ornate hawk eagle stands over the prey it just caught—a great green macaw.

Polisar and King were searching for tracks as evidence of big cats in the rain forest when they heard shrill shrieks. Along with the two soldiers who were with them, the pair hurried to the ravine just ahead where the sound was coming from.

Once they scrambled down into the ravine, they discovered a great green macaw and an ornate hawk eagle on the ground. The macaw was flapping fiercely as it struggled to reach the eagle's foot with its snapping beak. But the eagle's talon-grip kept its prey pressed so tightly to the ground the macaw couldn't attack.

Polisar said, "In the midst of this battle, the eagle looked straight at us like it was really angry and ready to defend its prey from us."

But even though great green macaws are listed as an endangered species, the scientists remained observers because they weren't in the rain forest to alter nature's predator and prey conflict. When the ornate hawk eagle won the battle, the scientists and the soldiers slipped away, leaving it to its meal.

More Exciting Discoveries

As scientists who studied large mammals, Polisar and King were excited to see lots of piglike white-lipped peccaries. Having been heavily hunted for food throughout Central America, this animal is endangered and rare elsewhere. The healthy population of peccaries here meant there was ample prey for large mammals, such as big cats. And, one day, while watching the peccaries, the scientists made an exciting discovery that proved them right.

King said, "We were following a family group [of peccaries] that were kind of like a train moving across a hillside, digging up all this plant material, which is great for the forest—opens it up for new plants to grow. And, all of a sudden, we're in the footsteps of a big cat because it's following them as well."

The scientists didn't see the cat that day, but they recognized the tracks as belonging to a puma. Polisar said, "Seeing it showed this [the Lost City site] was an

This is a puma footprint. The puma is the fourth largest of the world's big cats and the second largest in Central America, behind the jaguar.

White-lipped peccaries are about the size of a large dog and armed with sharp tusks.

intact ecosystem with an intact trophic [food] chain able to support the largest predators at the top. That was impressive because Central America doesn't have that many of those places left."

Medina-Fitoria, who focused on bats, made yet another big discovery. Every night, with the help of assistant Turcios-Casco, he set up a large mist net (strong, naturally baggy netting stretched between two support poles) in an area the bats were likely to swoop through. Then the pair checked the net about every fifteen minutes—just long enough for some bats to become trapped but not so long that their struggles could injure them. One by one, each captured bat was lifted out of the net, measured, identified, photographed, and released. And one night, one of the bats Medina-Fitoria caught was a pale-faced bat (*Phylloderma stenops*). This was the first recorded sighting of that kind of bat anywhere in Honduras since 1971.

Above: The pale-faced bat is so rare that little is known about its life other than that it eats fruit and insects. Arnulfo Medina-Fitoria was very excited to find it at the Lost City site.

Left: After he removed the bat from the net trap, Arnulfo Medina-Fitoria gently held it while he recorded information about it. Once finished, he released the bat.

Van den Berghe made four important discoveries about the animal life at the Lost City site. First, he investigated all the aquatic habitats, including fast-flowing streams, slow-flowing water along undercut stream banks, still water in streams, and pools of water. He identified thirteen species of fish that were only ever known to live in clean water. So, his first discovery was that the Lost City site was a healthy undisturbed forest where nothing polluted the water.

Van den Berghe made his second discovery while he was catching and identifying fish. He was very excited to find one fish that had a lot of the characteristics of a kind of fish called a molly (*Poecilia sphenops*). But it was different in some ways. And he caught three of those mollylike fish, proving this wasn't just a single, unusual fish. Later, back in his home laboratory while preparing to report on his expedition discoveries, he studied his field notes and preserved specimens of these unusual fish. Van den Berghe determined the type of molly living at the Lost City site really

Eric van den Berghe studied fish at the Lost City site by catching them with a seine net—a net with a weighted bottom that sinks so the net hangs vertically in the water until a line is tugged, closing the bottom of the net, and trapping the fish.

Mollies are small (about 4 inches [10 cm] long) algae-eating freshwater fish that give birth to live young rather than laying eggs. The kind of molly found at the Lost City site was different enough from other molly species that it was declared a brand-new species.

was different enough to be identified as a new kind of molly—a brand-new species.

Van den Berghe's third discovery at the Lost City site was an insect. One day, he investigated some holes in the ground and discovered they were burrows with tiger beetle larvae (developing young) inside. And these were the larvae of a species of tiger beetle (*Odontochila nicaraguense*) that had been believed extinct. He was unable to find any adult tiger beetles in the short time he had to look for them. But just finding the larvae meant that adults must be living in the area. So, that species wasn't extinct after all.

Then van den Berghe made his fourth discovery. He found a kind of longhorn beetle (*Ischnocnemis caerulescens*). That was amazing because, while this beetle was known to live elsewhere in Central America, it was the very first discovery of the species in Honduras.

Above: This is a male longhorn beetle. Males are bigger than females and have supersized jaws to battle other males for a mate.

Right: Lots of dobsonflies, like this one, were found at the Lost City site. Since this insect's larvae (young) need to be in clean water to develop, seeing them was proof this area was pristine.

A Close Encounter

For his part of the scientific study of the Lost City site, Larsen focused on insects. Although walking away from camp on his own at night wasn't a good idea, he sometimes did it anyway. He wanted to be as stealthy as possible to spot active nighttime insects in the beam of the headlight he wore.

One night, while investigating on his own, he walked into a narrow ravine between shoulder-high rock walls. While there, his light began to dim. Knowing he needed to return to camp, he started to turn around. Just as he moved his head, his headlight beam sliced through the dark and sparked a glow in a pair of eyes. Larsen said, "I figured it was about 30 feet [9.1 m] away and, though I couldn't see more than its eyes, I guessed it was a big cat. I could tell it was creeping closer, but I felt so excited seeing it I wasn't frightened—only curious."

The cat was clearly watching him too because its eyes continued to glow in the headlight's beam. Larsen said, "It kept coming until it was no more than eight feet [2.4 m] from me. I could see it clearly then. It was a puma! The cat and I stared at each other for a few seconds. Then it turned and bounded away from me down the ravine into the dark."

Larsen sucked in a breath as his curiosity evaporated and fear flooded through him. He had no idea where the puma was going. It could be running away. Or it could be headed to the top of the ravine's rock wall to jump down and attack him. He hiked back to camp as quickly as he could. There he joined a group sitting around the fire swapping stories of their day's adventures. No one was going to top the story he was about to tell.

Pumas have been recorded running as fast as 50 miles (80 km) per hour—a lot faster than any human can run.

Sneaky Snooping

Larsen's encounter with the puma made the RAP team members wonder what other animals they had not seen in the rain forest at night. They also wondered what wild animals had managed to avoid being spotted even by the scientists' careful observations during their daytime exploring. Luckily, the RAP team had a way to find out. They installed camera traps.

Each camera trap camera was only a little bigger than a standard cell phone, lightweight, and powered by lithium batteries capable of keeping it operating for as long as a year. Each camera used a black flash trigger, so it projected an infrared light beam (light in a range neither human nor animal vision could detect). Then any animal breaking that beam caused the camera to take its picture or, if set to video, briefly film it in action.

Travis King (*right*) readied a camera trap camera while Manfredo A. Turcios-Casco cleared away vines and brush. That tree was chosen as a camera trap site because it was on an animal highway—a path animal tracks showed wildlife regularly followed through the rain forest.

This is a daytime camera trap photo of a tapir. Although this animal looks something like a pig, it's related to rhinos.

03-31-2017 04:26:11 19°c

Some camera trap cameras used a normal bright flash at night, which though they likely startled the animals, captured color photos. Others used an infrared flash, which animals wouldn't notice, but took only black-and-white photos. King and Polisar were responsible for setting up the camera trap sites, and they installed twenty-two cameras—each strapped to a tree at about their knee-level.

King said, "I need to know that the camera trap will work. So, once it's in place, I take off my backpack and crawl past it like a cat. Sometimes, I get all the way down to be as low as a rat or an otter. If the little red light on the camera goes off, I know it's taken my picture." Then King felt certain the camera trap would photograph any passing animal.

Although the camera traps were active as soon as they were installed, the photos and videos they captured wouldn't be available to the RAP team for months. Because of the dense rain forest canopy, camera traps couldn't transmit images via satellite. Instead, someone would have to return to the Lost City site to collect the cameras. So, as each camera trap was installed, its GPS location was recorded on a map to make recovering it possible.

Finally, all that remained to do was pack up the camping equipment, research equipment, and any collected specimens. The RAP team also collected any trash they had created during their stay because the scientists were determined to leave the Lost City site as untouched as possible. And they left the way they'd arrived—ferried away from the rain forest by helicopter.

This freshwater crab was in its defensive pose when it was photographed.

This is a nighttime camera trap photo of a red brocket deer. Notice the camera trap photo was automatically stamped with the date, exact time, and air temperature. Some cameras recorded the temperature in Celsius and some in Fahrenheit.

🌡 83°F   ○ 04/26/2017   06:35PM   TK001

It was time to review everything and report on the condition of the ecosystems they'd explored and the plants and animals they'd discovered at the Lost City site. But before the scientists could do that, they needed to be able to study the camera trap photos and videos. Whatever the camera traps captured would be the only opportunity to observe the area's wildlife when no human intruders were around. So, who would go back to recover the camera trap cameras?

Dangerous Recovery Mission

The plan had been for someone to return to the Lost City site for the camera trap cameras in April 2017, just two months after the RAP team's expedition. But Honduran politics and funding problems delayed approval for the recovery mission until August.

Concerned a further delay could happen, RAP team leader Larsen decided he needed to act quickly. He asked Turcios-Casco to go after the cameras because he lived in Honduras. He had also been an assistant during the RAP team expedition, so he was familiar with the Lost City site. Turcios-Casco accepted the job and was ferried back to the Lost City site by helicopter on September 2, 2017.

Turcios-Casco took along a GPS locator and the map with the GPS coordinates for each of the camera traps. He would camp at the same site as before and share it with a Honduran archaeological group. But he was only funded for the in-and-out flights, four days of camping supplies, and just three Honduran soldiers to provide support.

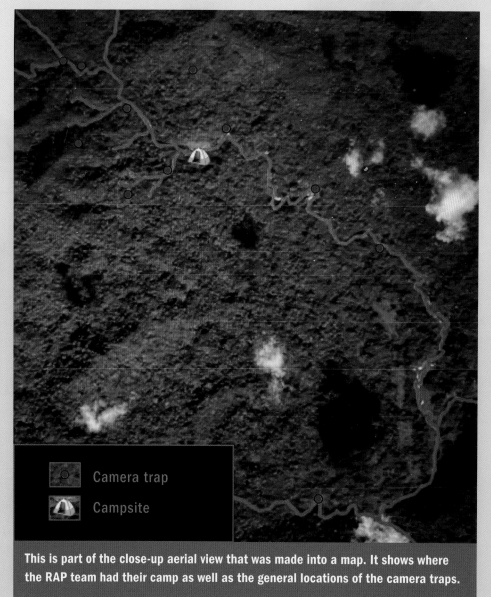

Camera trap

Campsite

This is part of the close-up aerial view that was made into a map. It shows where the RAP team had their camp as well as the general locations of the camera traps.

The search and recovery effort also proved to be very difficult. Climbing up steep, slippery slopes was an exhausting struggle. Wading through streams was still possible in some places and preferable to hacking a path through the thick undergrowth, but it wasn't easy.

All too often, sections of streams were suddenly chest deep. While wading, he often brushed against thorny plants that tore holes in his jeans until they were so ragged he cut off the pant legs, making them shorts. The downside to this was that his legs were cut by the thorny vegetation, and he often had to stop to pick off ticks.

September was the rainy season in La Mosquitia, so the forest was always dripping wet, muddy, and swarming with mosquitoes and sand flies. There was also the danger of flash floods.

Reaching a camera trap location also wasn't the end of the search. Even with the soldiers helping, it took Turcios-Casco at least an hour and often more than two hours to find each camera. So much time had passed that the fast-growing rain forest plants covered the cameras. And sometimes all the searching was for nothing. Turcios-Casco found the site where camera 3 had been attached. But the plants there looked dragged as if a flood had swept through. Perhaps the camera was swept away because he never found it. While the loss of that camera was disappointing, finding camera 21 missing was shocking. Someone had likely stolen it because the camera was gone, but the tape used to anchor it to the tree was still there. Camera 11 suffered a similar fate although only its memory card was taken.

Manfredo A. Turcios-Casco was surprised during a lunch break by a small wild cat, a jaguarundi, that jumped from a tree to the ground near him.

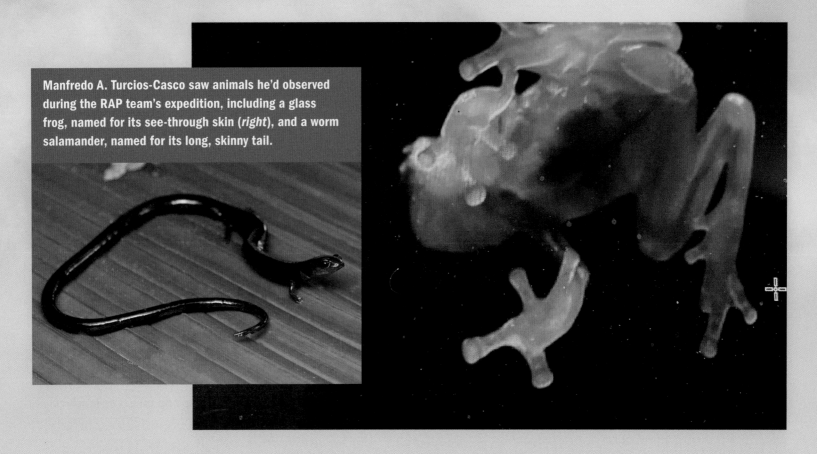

Manfredo A. Turcios-Casco saw animals he'd observed during the RAP team's expedition, including a glass frog, named for its see-through skin (*right*), and a worm salamander, named for its long, skinny tail.

Each night back in camp, Turcios-Casco recorded the day's animal sightings and his efforts to locate camera traps in a notebook. While each report recounted facing great challenges, none would equal what happened on his third day at the Lost City site. While walking in a stream, he was swept away by a flash flood. Being close to the stream bank, he grabbed onto plants to anchor himself. Then, fighting the current, he hauled himself to safety. Turcios-Casco said, "By the time I climbed ashore, some of my equipment and food was lost. But, by luck, I didn't lose the GPS [locator] or the map. So, I could keep looking for camera traps."

By the time his four-day mission was over, Turcios-Casco had recovered nineteen of the twenty-two cameras. So, what did the camera trap photos and videos reveal? And what final report did the RAP team make?

Wild Secrets Revealed

The camera trap cameras delivered fourteen thousand images, letting the RAP team scientists see some animals they had not spotted during the expedition. That included the jaguar, though they'd often seen this big cat's fresh tracks close to their campsite. The date and time stamp on a photo of peccaries followed closely by the photo of a jaguar proved this predator was tracking them. That was proof this location had a healthy food chain.

After all the camera trap photos and videos were studied, that information was added to the data the RAP team scientists collected while they were at the Lost City site. Then the totals of all the plant and animal species they'd discovered there were compiled on a chart. This accompanied written reports focused on the plants and each of the different groups of animals the scientists studied, including birds, butterflies, arthropods (such as spiders), reptiles, amphibians, fish, small mammals (such as bats), medium-sized mammals (such as peccaries), and large mammals (such as jaguars).

After only seeing this big cat's tracks while they were in the rain forest, the scientists were thrilled to see this camera trap photo of a jaguar hunting at the Lost City site.

Category	Total	New to Honduras	Threatened	New species
Plants	183	3	14	0
Orchids	19	0	0	0
Butterflies/moths	246	15	0	0
Other arthropods	XX*	3	1	0
Fishes	13	0	0	1
Amphibians	22	0	4	0
Reptiles	35	0	8	0
Birds	198	0	9	0
Rodents	10	0	0	0
Bats	30	1	1	0
Large mammals	30	0	6	0
Total	**786**	**22**	**43**	**1**

*This table created by the RAP team for their expedition report lists the kinds of animals and plants investigated and the number of different species discovered for each category except *Other arthropods*. Trond Larsen explained the team observed a great many examples of other arthropods during their investigation of the Lost City site. So they decided to include only the few other arthropods that were really striking and noteworthy. Those were the ones new to Honduras and the one threatened species.

The city ruins in La Mosquitia were officially named the City of the Jaguar because of an ancient artifact. Seeing photos of that big cat there tied the past to the present and inspired efforts to protect the site for the future.

The RAP team report showed that the variety of plants and animals thriving at the Lost City site in La Mosquitia was exceptional. Such diversity was only ever found within pristine, intact ecosystems. That meant there were plants to support various plant eaters that would in turn provide food for a variety of small, medium, and even large predators. Most exciting was the discovery of several animals listed as endangered. These included healthy populations of great green macaws, Geoffroy's spider monkeys, and Baird's tapirs.

Then there were the three amazing discoveries of animals believed extinct but rediscovered alive at the Lost City site: the pale-faced bat, the false tree coral snake, and the tiger beetle. And the scientists investigating the water habitats at the Lost City site discovered one totally new species of fish, a kind of molly.

Archaeologist Chris Fisher was willing to push through some of nature's fiercest challenges to explore the Lost City site in La Mosquitia.

The discovery expedition and the archaeology expedition established the historical value of this area of La Mosquitia rain forest. The RAP team's expedition confirmed it was also an important conservation site. Rare and threatened animals still thrived there. And it was home to healthy populations of animals that were becoming increasingly scarce elsewhere. Its towering, ancient trees and totally unpolluted water made it valuable. But how could such a remote rain forest area be guarded against the threat of humans intruding to steal ancient artifacts, cut valuable timber, or illegally hunt animals, especially rare and valuable ones, such as jaguars?

In 2018 the Honduran government launched the Kaha Kamasa Foundation (named for White City in the Miskito language) to focus on patrolling to protect the Lost City site and the surrounding area of La Mosquitia rain forest. As a result of the RAP team's report, Global Wildlife Conservation and the Wildlife Conservation Society partnered with this group committing to long-term

Imagine how excited the RAP team scientists were to discover this false tree coral snake, previously believed extinct in Honduras.

This daytime camera trap photo of a peccary family at home in the Lost City site is an amazing peek at this pristine rain forest ecosystem.

financial support for protecting the Lost City site. Larsen said, "Hopefully, our report will remain a record of what is living there and not a record of what once existed."

Indeed, the real secret of the Lost City isn't that people, long ago, lived in that part of La Mosquitia.

It's that this site is one of Earth's remaining pristine places—somewhere still free of plastic trash and where an amazing variety of plants and animals thrive. That's a secret worth keeping!

A Note from Sandra Markle

Secrets of the Lost City is without a doubt the most fascinating science detective story I've ever tackled. In fact, it's not just one but three intertwined adventures. I was honored to talk with a number of those involved.

Sadly, some members of each of the expeditions suffered health problems afterward. For example, Trond Larsen had to be treated for blistering skin eruptions caused by parasites tunneling under his skin. And a number of people suffered symptoms of leishmaniasis. However, everyone who went on the expeditions knew beforehand that they were going to a very challenging environment and they went anyway. After all, each of the expeditions was the opportunity of a lifetime. First, to be part of discovering the Lost City. Next to share in investigating what the people who once lived there left behind. Then to learn about the plants and animals, some of them unique, currently living there.

The expeditions to the Lost City site in La Mosquitia proved that with the help of science, we can still find and explore amazing places on our planet. What is important for the future is that we choose to value such places enough to use science and technology to study them without damaging them and that

we resist exploiting them. Such pristine tropical rain forests are Earth's lifeboats in the flood of global climate change. They not only take in and store carbon dioxide, but they also release oxygen—and both are important for Earth's ecosystems to thrive. So we need to do our very best to let pristine places, such as the Lost City site, remain so untouched that there isn't even any plastic to be found there.

Glossary

anthropologist: a person who studies people and their ancestors in relation to their environment and social interactions

archaeologist: a person who explores human history and people before recorded history by studying sites where they lived, artifacts they left, and even human remains

artifact: an object made or shaped by humans that often provides insights into the customs and lives of the people

biologist: a person who studies the natural world and things living in it, including plants and animals

camera trap: a camera that uses a motion sensor or light beam as a trigger to snap a picture, capturing wild animals on film without people being present

ecosystem: an interconnected community of plants and animals

endangered: a species facing a high risk of extinction

extinct: a species that no longer has any living members

GPS (Global Positioning System): a system of navigation in which satellites circle Earth and constantly send signals that are picked up by a receiver that calculates distances from four or more of these satellites to compute its exact location on Earth

habitat: an animal's home area that supplies the food, water, and shelter it needs to live plus the place it can raise its young

lidar (light detection and ranging): using pulsed laser light to measure varying distances to Earth in order to produce 3D maps of Earth's surface and features on it

mammal: warm-blooded, hairy animal whose females nurse their young

pristine: unspoiled condition, as though untouched by people

remote: a place far from where people live

species: a kind of living thing

specimen: an individual plant or animal collected for scientific study

tropical rain forest: a hot, humid forest near the equator with tall, densely growing, broad-leaved evergreen trees in an area of high annual rainfall

Source Notes

8   Steve Elkins, interview with author, November 11, 2020.

11   Steve Elkins, interview with author, September 3, 2021.

14   Chris Fisher, interview with author, November 16, 2020.

17   Elkins, interview, September 3, 2021.

17   Fisher, interview, November 16, 2020.

18   Chris Fisher, interview with author, September 9, 2021.

19   Fisher.

19   Fisher.

21   Fisher.

21   Fisher.

25   Travis King, interview with author, May 29, 2020.

29   John Polisar, interview with author, June 1, 2020.

30   Travis King, interview with author, February 4, 2021.

30–31   Polisar, interview.

34   Trond Larsen, interview with author, May 29, 2020.

34   Larsen.

37   King, interview, February 4, 2021.

43   Manfredo A. Turcios-Casco, interview with author, November 25, 2020.

49   Larsen, interview.

Explore More

To find out even more, check out the following books and websites:

Books

De la Bedoyere, Camilla. *100 Facts Rainforest*. Thaxted, UK: Miles Kelly, 2019. Stunning photos and amazing facts plus quizzes and activities make learning about rain forests fun.

Delano, Marfé Ferguson. *Explore My World Rainforests*. Washington, DC: National Geographic Kids, 2017. Explore this majestic part of the world and the animals and plants living there.

Markle, Sandra. *Woolly Monkey Mysteries: The Quest to Save a Rain Forest Species*. Minneapolis: Millbrook Press, 2019. Join scientists installing extraordinary numbers of camera traps high in trees to investigate and try to save monkeys that play a key role in the rain forest ecosystem.

Messner, Kate. *Over and Under the Rainforest*. San Francisco: Chronicle Books, 2020. Discover the wonder of the tropical rain forest from the canopy to its roots.

Websites

Camera Trapping for Conservation
https://www.wwf.org.uk/project/conservationtechnology/camera-trap
Check out this World Wildlife Fund's overview of the history of camera traps and how they are a powerful conservation tool. Then view WWF camera trap photos from around the world at https://wwf.panda.org/discover/our_focus/wildlife_practice/camera_traps/.

Lidar
https://www.explainthatstuff.com/lidar.html
Explore how lidar works, what it does, and how it's changing how we navigate the world.

The Lost City of the Monkey God
https://www.youtube.com/watch?v=zoYheMMTa-0
This is the official trailer for the documentary filmed about the discovery expedition, which is currently available through online streaming sites.

"What Are the Layers of the Rainforest?"
https://www.youtube.com/watch?v=eh5vIBKIEQM
Watch this quick YouTube trip from the rain forest floor to the canopy top.

Index

Photo Acknowledgments

Image credits: Lucian Read courtesy of Benenson Productions, p. 4; The American Weekly/ Wikimedia Commons (public domain), p. 6 (all); © Dave Yoder/National Geographic, pp. 7, 10, 12, 13, 14–15, 16, 18, 19, 20, 21, 47; Marion Renk-Richardson courtesy of Steve Elkins, p. 8; © Figure(s) created by Dr. Juan Carlos Fernandez-Diaz of the National Center for Airborne Laser Mapping (NCALM) based on data collected for Under The Lidar (UTL) Productions, pp. 9 (bottom left), (bottom right), 11; © Douglas Preston, p. 17; © Trond Larsen, pp. 22, 23 (all), 25, 26 (left, bottom), 27 (all), 30 (all), 31 (right), 32 (top), 33 (all), 38, 40, 43 (all), 48; adrian hepworth/Alamy Stock Photo, p. 24; © Eric van den Berghe, p. 26 (top); © John Polisar, pp. 28, 46; © The Mammal Spatial Ecology and Conservation Lab of Washington State University, Wildlife Conservation Society, Panthera, Zamorano University, Honduran Forest Conservation Institute, Conservation International, Travis King, John Polisar, Manfredo Turcios, pp. 31 (left), 36, 37, 39, 44, 49; © Nick Hawkins/ NPL/Minden Pictures, pp. 34–35; ORLANDO SIERRA/AFP/Getty Images, p. 41; Rolf Nussbaumer Photography/Alamy Stock Photo, p. 42; Julie Larsen Maher © WCS 46; Skip Jeffery Photography, p. 50.

Cover: jamenpercy/iStock/Getty Images; Dan Antoche-Albisor/500px/Getty Images; JOGENDRA KUMAR/Shutterstock.com.